Living for Christ

A Call to Holy Living and Sacrifice

Joshua Dykes

GOSPEL TRAVELER
Ambassadors for Christ

Self Published by Joshua Dykes with the help of Amazon publishing tools

This book may not be reproduced or sold in any format (paper or electronic) without the written permission of the author, signed with his signature. Up to a quarter of the book can be printed and used (for class or evangelistic purposes only) without permission from the author, given that an entire chapter of the book is not quoted. **Requests for reproduction can be made through the website address listed below.** By opening this book (in any format), you have agreed to these terms and conditions.

www.gospeltraveler.com

Scripture quotations marked CSB have been taken from the Christian Standard Bible ®, Copyright © 2017 by Holman Bible Publishers. Used by permission. Christian Standard Bible ® and CSB ® are federally registered trademarks of Holman Bible Publishers.

Edited by Jewell July
Cover Design by Saya Eagleman

** The author has chosen to leave the 'c' in church of Christ as lower case because of personal conviction and preference.

Dedicated to Central church of Christ in Decaturville, TN.

I am thankful to have served as your Associate Minister and I am encouraged by your support and patience. To my wonderful Bible class students who have done so well and have learned so much, I hope you continue to walk in the statutes and commands of our LORD and Savior Jesus Christ - every day, living for Him.

My students: Anna, Chandler, Chelsea, and HaLee.

A special dedication goes to my dad and mom, an elder and an elder's wife.

TABLE OF CONTENTS

Note from the Author..5
Paul's Radical Change..6
Dying in Sin...11
Chasing Riches..17
Consuming 'Much' Wine..22
Little Calves..28
Lingering in Our Comfort Zones...............................33
Focusing on Self..37
Dying to Sin...41
Chasing Christ...47
Consuming God's Word..52
Focusing on Others..56
Jumping Out of Our Comfort Zones..........................60
Your Radical Change..64
Exegetical Approach to Philippians 1:20-30..............67
About the Author...79

Note from the Author

I commend and thank you for choosing to pick up a copy of this book to read! I have spent many months studying, writing, and editing to produce the book that you have in your hands; and I could not be more happy that you have chosen this book.

If you read this book, I ask that you do not merely skim it or breeze over the passages quoted. I ask that you read diligently and with an intent to learn more about Christ and what it means to live for Him.

It is my hope and honest prayer that my words and the Words of the Lord (which are quoted within) will bring you much joy and encouragement.

In Him,
Joshua C. Dykes

1

Paul's Radical Change

One evening as I was scrolling through my Facebook feed, I came upon a birthday post for a one hundred and eighty-eight year old tortoise named Jonathan. My first thought was one of astonishment and surprise. And I had an immediate desire to show my dad. So that is exactly what I did. When I showed him the picture of Jonathan and explained to him that it was his 188th birthday, he said, "Imagine all that tortoise would have seen in its lifetime if it were human." How true that is! If we were 188 years old, having seen everything between then and now, how much differently would we be living our current lives?

Let us say that we lived over 2000 years ago and we got to experience the life of Christ and the ministry of the apostles. We got to see all the miracles and hear all the teachings of Jesus. We got to see his birth, his ministry, his death, and his resurrection. We got to see his ascension into heaven. We got to see the persecution and their brave zeal of the apostles. How much differently would we be living our lives having seen what they had seen?

In the Bible, we read of a man who lived his life one way but changed radically. The man's name is Paul. Paul has to be the second most fascinating character in the New Testament, behind Jesus. His conversion story and post-conversion life are evidence of the truth in Christianity. After all, how could one so opposed to Christianity change his life in such a way that he becomes one of the most radical missionaries ever recorded?

The radicalism of Paul is made most evident in Philippians 1:21 in which he describes the purpose of his life following his conversion:

"For me, to live is Christ and to die is gain." (All verses are taken from the CSB unless otherwise noted).

This verse of just a few words packs a powerful message from Paul. To better understand the radicalism of this verse, we must first look at his life before conversion and after it. There are three passages in the book of Acts that reveal the narrative of Paul's conversion: Acts 9, Acts 22, and Acts 26. Two of these conversion accounts are told by Paul himself. These passages illustrate the intensity of the changes Paul made in his life.

The road to Damascus is where Paul started his radical change. Paul was on his way to persecute more Christians; that is what he was known for. But something happened on that road to Damascus. Paul, being blinded by the glory of Christ, was commanded to go into Damascus and wait for further instruction. Ananias, another devout Jew, was commanded by the Lord to restore Paul's sight and tell him everything that he must do for the Kingdom. After Ananias restored Paul's vision, this is what he told Paul his post-conversion life was supposed to consist of:

> Acts 22:14-16
>
> "*And he said, 'The God of our ancestors has appointed you to know his will, to see the Righteous One, and to hear the words from his mouth, since you will be a witness for him to all people of what you have seen and heard. And now, why are you delaying? Get up and be baptized, and wash away your sins, calling on his name'.*" (CSB)

Paul was called to be a 'witness for him'. Who is the 'him' that Paul was called to witness for? He was called to be a witness for Christ. Christ was the very reason why Paul was called to suffer many things. God saw that Paul's zeal would help to grow the Church, even in the midst of persecution. As a matter of fact, Paul is so zealous, that the very reason he wishes to live is so Christ can continue to be proclaimed (Phil. 1:21).

Prior to seeing the glory of Christ on the road to Damascus, he already had a reputation for being a persecutor of the church (Acts 8:1-3). The Jews entrusted him with the task of stopping the spread of Christianity (Acts 7:58). Why did they give him such a task? Paul had met many qualifications that proved he was zealous for Judaism:

- He was born of the tribe of Benjamin (Phil. 3:5). The Tribe of Benjamin was one of only two tribes to remain mostly loyal to Judaism. After all, Benjamin was part of the southern kingdom (Judah) which was more righteous than its northern neighbor.

- In regards to the Old Law, he was seen as 'blameless' (Phil. 3:6). Other Jews saw him as a leader and they cast their garments upon his feet at the stoning of Steven (Acts 7).

- He was a pupil of Gamaliel, a great Jewish teacher (Acts. 22:3). So his knowledge of the Law would have been superior to most Jews.

Understanding Paul's radical zeal for the Jewish faith is crucial for Christians. His life is one (of many) proofs that we have in defense of Christianity. How could he be so zealous and stubborn for his faith, being known a persecutor of the church, and eventually become a convert to the very faith he was trying to destroy? Radical change occurred in the life of Paul.

Throughout the rest of this book, we will talk about what it means to live a life that revolves around Christ. **If your life does not revolve around Christ and if he is not central in your life, then maybe it is time for a radical change.**

DISCUSSION QUESTIONS

1. What does it mean to be a 'radical Christian'?

2. Paul heard his calling to go and be a witness for Christ. Have we also been called to be a witness? If yes, give a verse that shows how we have been called.

3. The fact that Paul was from the tribe of Benjamin was a proof for his zealousness for Judaism. What is significant about the tribe of Benjamin?

4. Is repentance from one's former life a radical change that must occur?

2
Dying in Sin

If one wants to begin living for Christ, it might be important to observe what living is not. The first thing that we need to understand is that 'Living for Christ' is not continuing to live in sin. The Bible tells us on numerous occasions that sin will only lead to future destruction. The punishment of death has become the sentence for our crimes against God.

What makes sin dangerous to the Christian? Well, sin is defined in Isaiah 59:2 as that which 'separates us from God'. If God is the source of life (Gen. 2:7), then distancing ourselves from Him certainly means death.

In Genesis 3, following the temptation of Eve and the fall of the human race, God tells Adam the consequence for eating the forbidden fruit:

> Genesis 3:19
>
> *"You will eat bread by the sweat of your brow until you return to the ground, since you were taken from it. For you are dust, and you will return to dust."*

What God is telling Adam is that they have now introduced death into the world as a result of their sin. If they had not eaten of the forbidden fruit, then Adam and Eve and all their descendants would still be living in the Garden of Eden, in harmony with God.

In Leviticus 10, Nadab and Abihu offered profane fire before the Lord (which went against the statutes given in Leviticus 6:12-13). As a result of their sin, the fiery fury of God's wrath consumed them and they were struck dead.

There are many more examples given in the Old Testament of physical death being a consequence to sin. However, Spiritual death should be far more feared. The wages of sin committed in this life result in death in the next (Rom. 6:23). Many books have been written on the subject of hell and death in the second life. It is not the goal of this book to discuss such a subject, but the study of such a place is often vanity. The torment one faces in hell cannot be comprehended, but it can be avoided by living righteously (Rev. 21:8).

Perhaps the worst movie I have ever read or heard about (it sounded so terrible that I could not bear to watch it) is *Wolf of Wall-Street*. I have never seen this movie because of the pornography and the alienating language that I heard exists within it; however, the most condensed summary of the movie I can come up with is 'a guy lives to satisfy his lusts, but loses his soul in the process'. He scams people out of money and uses the money to live the 'rich life'. I remember my mother telling me about the movie after she watched it, and she told me that the main character made himself pitiful.

I guess we could say that King Solomon lived a similar lifestyle. He had over seven-hundred wives and concubines and had given himself over to enjoying the pleasures that they could provide rather than looking to God for satisfaction. As a result, he ended up giving in to their idolatry (1 Kin. 11:1-4). However, he understood that seeking satisfaction in pleasure(s) was futile (Ecc. 2).

As was mentioned previously, sin comes as a result of seeking satisfaction in pleasure(s) or giving in to what entices our eyes. Temptation is personal and is different for each person (Jam. 1:14). We realize that if we do not allow God to fight our spiritual battles, we will lose and we will give in to our sins. And because sins are a result of giving in to our temptations, we must understand that our thoughts and our hearts are corrupted. All to often, I have heard prosperity gospel preachers say the following:

- *"God just wants you to be happy."*
- *"God loves you and he wants you to follow your heart."*
- *"If you have a gut feeling, it is from the Spirit and you need to listen."*

What these preachers fail to understand is that the Bible presents two different mindsets. Both of these mindsets can be seen in Romans 8.

> Romans 8:5-8
>
> "*For those who live according to the flesh have their **minds set** on the things of the **flesh**, but those who live according to the Spirit have their minds set on the things of the Spirit. Now the **mind-set of the flesh is death**, but the mind-set of the Spirit is life and peace. The **mind-set of the flesh is hostile to God** because it does not submit to God's law. Indeed, it is unable to do so. **Those who are in the flesh cannot please God.**"

In this passage, we see a contrast between the mindset of the flesh and the mindset of the Spirit. Those who live in sin do so because that is what their mind is set on. If a church were to listen to the advice of these prosperity gospel preachers, then we can be sure that they will fall into sin.

A couple of years ago, I had the privilege of studying with some Mormons. I wanted to know more about Mormonism, and who better to ask than someone who was brought up in that faith. I had asked them to tell me why they believe the Book of Mormon, Doctrines and Covenants, and the Pearl of Great Price to be inspired by God. They replied that all I had to do was read the Book of Mormon and pray to God. If I did these two things, then I could know that the Book of Mormon was true. We know that it is sin to add to the Gospel (Gal. 1:8-10), but the Mormons had rejected this notion and decided to follow their own hearts rather than the knowledge revealed in the Word of God. Solomon said it well in Proverbs 14:12, and this seems to sum up how we should view our heart's desires.

> **Proverbs 14:12**
>
> *"There is a way that seems right to a person, but its end is the way to death."*

Often times people sin unintentionally, and I do believe that many people who believe heretical teachings are sincere in their faith (the same could be said for Jehovah's Witnesses and other denominations who follow the teachings and doctrines of men). However, there are people that sin intentionally. They plot evil against the Lord. Their minds are set on the things of the flesh, and they **know** it is. One such figure was Judas Iscariot. He knew that he was going to be the one to betray Jesus, yet he did it anyways. Although the Lord knew that Judas was going to do it, he had freewill and he could have avoided it. However, he let his love for money replace his love for the Lord (Matt. 26:21-25). If one sins willfully, he/she neglects Jesus Christ as their sacrifice and has no covering after this life (Heb. 10:26). As a result, they will perish.

DISCUSSION QUESTIONS

1. What makes sin dangerous to the Christian?

2. Why should we want to avoid sinning?

3. Read **Romans 3:23** and answer the following questions:

    A. Have you sinned?

    B. Do you feel as if you 'fall short' of pleasing God?

4. If something feels right, should you do it? Why or why not?

5. Read **Ephesians 2:1-2**. After having read this passage, how does this make you feel?

3
Chasing Riches

The world often says that you cannot be happy unless you have a lot of money. I cannot overstate how many times I have seen individuals work their lives away, all so they can ensure they 'get rich' and buy happiness. Here are two real quotes that I have read of secular minds sharing their view of money:

> "The money you make is a symbol of the value you create."

> "People say that money is not the key to happiness, but I always figured if you have enough money, you can have a key made."

The latter quote I found to be more humorous; however, both of these quotes still show the flawed perception the world has of money. The world's faulty perceptions are **ALWAYS** in contrast to the wisdom found in scripture.

The world teaches greed. The Bible teaches generosity.

The world teaches taking. The Bible teaches giving.

The world teaches 'get more and you'll be happy'. The Bible teaches 'be content with what you have and count them as blessings'.

In Paul's epistles, he reveals the many dangers of money. He also reveals key information on how Christians are to view material objects. This is perhaps best seen in 1 Timothy 6:7-10.

> 1 Timothy 6:7-10
>
> *"For we brought nothing into the world, and we can take nothing out. If we have food and clothing, we will be content with these. But those who want to be rich fall into temptation, a trap, and many foolish and harmful desires, which plunge people into ruin and destruction. For the love of money is a root of all kinds of evil, and by craving it, some have wandered away from the faith and pierced themselves with many griefs."* (CSB)

Nothing that was made in this world will be carried into the next. Here we see a line drawn between the physical realm and the spiritual realm. In the physical realm, people are anxious and they worry about material matters that are not at all related to their spiritual well-being. In his letter to Timothy, Paul warns of the dangers of material wealth. We have all heard the expression, "Mo' money, mo' problems!" This expression is so true. With more money does come more problems and more temptations.

There are so many instances of individuals who have chased riches, but have ended up either working away their entire lives or gambling away all of their possessions. They do this hoping that they can be fully satisfied with their wealth, but we know that is never the case. The carnally minded individual believes that he/she can be fully satisfied with things of this world, but the spiritually minded individual will be **content** with whatever he/she has. The spiritually minded individual also knows that chasing riches is something that is ultimately vanity - it is something that Paul understood and it is something that Solomon also understood:

> Ecclesiastes 5:10-12
>
> *"The one who loves silver is **never satisfied** with silver, and whoever loves wealth is never satisfied with income. This too is **futile**. When good things increase, the ones who consume them multiply; what, then, is the profit to the owner, except to gaze at them with his eyes? The sleep of the worker is sweet, whether he eats little or much, but the abundance of the rich permits him no sleep."* (CSB)

When Solomon writes Ecclesiastes, he is writing this at an old age near the end of his life. God had given him all the knowledge and wisdom that he asked for (1 Kin. 3). Solomon, at a younger age, was a very faithful king and was obedient to the Lord. However, Solomon failed to apply godly wisdom and he married many Pagan women. These women led Solomon down a path of idolatry, evil, and greed. He possessed the wisdom to know the futility of riches, but it wasn't until after he experienced the personal emptiness and ultimate uselessness of riches that he decided to make a change late in his life. Paul understood that nothing in this material world can be carried into the next; therefore, a life dedicated to chasing riches is ultimately futile.

God's people have not been called to be 'zealous money chasers,' but to be 'generous money givers'.

Christians have also been called to be 'content' with what they have. Paul writes *"if we have food and clothing, we will be content with these"* (1 Tim. 6:8). What is contentment and what all does it entail? How can Christians be content with what they have, even if what they have is very little? I think the first passage we need to turn to in regards to contentment is Philippians 4:11-13. Verse 13 is a favorite verse of many, but they often do not know the context surrounding it. The entire chapter is wholesome and shows the amazing contentment Paul had in the midst of difficult circumstances (keep in mind, Paul wrote the letter of Philippians while he was in prison). However, this chapter also gives the very definition of contentment:

> Philippians 4:11-13
>
> *"I don't say this out of need, for I have learned to be content in whatever circumstances I find myself. I know both how to make do with little, and I know how to make do with a lot. In any and all circumstances I have learned the secret of being content - whether well fed or hungry, whether in abundance or in need. I am able to do all things through him who strengthens me."* (CSB)

If one is **truly content**, then it will not matter how much or little he/she possesses. The secret does not lie in trying to buy happiness, but being happy with the things you have already been blessed with. I am not saying that you should starve yourself or become poor, but I want to emphasize the point that living for possessions should not be the purpose of your life. Paul's secret to contentment - God provides us with all we need in this life, so let us focus more on the reward we will gain after. "For me to live is Christ, **and to die is gain**." Living for riches is futile and temporary, but living for Christ is future gain.

DISCUSSION QUESTIONS

1. The world and the Bible are always at odds with each other. Name some specific teachings in which they are at odds.

2. Jesus also taught that man should not be so anxious about the things of this world. Can you name any particular instances of Jesus teaching this?

3. What are some ways in which money can corrupt our souls and tempt us?

4. The Bible tells us that we are to be 'content'. What is contentment and how can we (as Christians) be more content?

5. If someone offered you a million dollars for your soul, would you be willing to sell it (please take this question seriously)? Why or why not?

4

Consuming 'Much' Wine

The name of this chapter may have caught you off-guard. You might be asking, "What does the consumption of wine (or the lack thereof) have to do with one's ability to 'live for Christ'?" I would argue that it has a lot to do with living for Christ. For many years, I have struggled answering questions concerning drinking and the consumption of alcohol. I think a lot of my struggle came from the fact that I wasn't really sure how I felt about it myself. However, I heard a sermon by Jeff May, a prominent minister in the church of Christ, that absolutely changed my attitude[1]. What he said in this sermon made me **absolutely sure** that the Christian should avoid alcohol (except for medicinal reasons). In this chapter, I will be using many of the points from his sermon to make the case why alcohol should be avoided. The first verse that proves that a Christian should stay away from alcohol is Hebrews 5:13-14.

> Hebrews 5:13-14
>
> *"Now everyone who lives on milk is inexperienced with the message about righteousness, because he is an infant. But solid food is for the mature - for those whose senses have been trained to distinguish between good and evil."* (CSB)

---

[1] The sermon can be found on churchofchristatoakland.com. The name of the sermon is called "The Christian and Alcohol" and it was preached on May 12, 2019. I highly recommend listening to this sermon.

Now I realize that this passage says nothing about alcohol, but it does talk about the importance of having a mind that can distinguish between good and evil. One of the many problems with alcohol is that it diminishes one's senses and makes them unaware of their actions. Christians have been called to be self-aware and to be wise in their actions. Why should Christians be wise in their actions? This is not a call for individuals to try to 'raise their IQ levels' or to 'have a good education'. It is a call to be 'sober minded' and spiritually mature.

What does it mean to be sober-minded? Dictionaries often tie the phrase to the **avoidance of alcohol or drunkenness**. The Merriam-Webster Dictionary has four different definitions for 'sober', but its fourth definition stands out: a sober-minded individual is "marked by temperance, moderation, or seriousness". In 1 Peter 1:13, Peter states that a Christian should have their 'minds ready for action, sober-minded'. This is the attitude that Christians are expected to have. One who is not sober has a mind marked by anger, instability, and stupidity. Christians should possess none of these qualities.

Jeff May also expressed his frustration in his sermon at the amount of preachers who are okay with members of their congregation drinking. I will not be able to express my frustration as clearly as Jeff May (mainly because it is more difficult to do in writing), but I assure you that I am just as frustrated - if not more so - than he is. I do not understand how one can be a preacher - a defender of the Gospel of Christ Jesus - and defend the practice of social drinking. I know that by saying that, I have probably turned a lot of people off from reading the rest of this book. I know it comes across as 'harsh', but I say it all in love. We live in a world of 'absolutes'. Either something is absolutely right or something is absolutely wrong. For the rest of this chapter, I will discuss the danger alcohol poses and why it shouldn't be consumed EXCEPT for medicinal purposes as outlined in scripture. Here are some 'evidences' that many give as to why the consumption of alcohol is acceptable:

1. Jesus did it.

2. Deacons are told to avoid drinking 'much wine'. So only the excess is forbidden.

3. Timothy was told to drink wine for his 'frequent illnesses'.

The first claim that will be combated is the false claim that Jesus drank socially. John 2:1-11 is the popular account in which we see Jesus turn water into wine. There are many things that we need to consider about this passage, the first of which is the occasion. This was a wedding feast. After all, there was a 'master of the feast' appointed to ensure that all went well with the feast. Not only was this a wedding, it was a Jewish wedding. Since this was a Jewish wedding, we know that Jewish laws regarding alcohol consumption would have been enforced, thus the alcohol content was very low, if any. They were not drinking for a buzz nor were they drinking to get drunk, because it would have been outside the nature of Christ to put a stumbling block in front of others by turning water into wine. Therefore, we can infer that the wine made by Christ was either void or low in alcohol content.

The second claim that will be combated is the one concerning deacons being commanded to avoid drinking 'much wine'. In 1 Timothy 3:2-4, Paul gives a list of qualifications and expectations of deacons (appointed workers of the congregation by a committee of elders). Among these qualifications is that he should not be given to 'much wine', or as the CSB translates, 'excessive drinking'. Many take that and often say things like, "well the excess of alcoholic beverages is forbidden, so a little is alright," or "it is only wrong if one becomes a drunkard".

However, there is much danger in saying that. Someone who is given to something is addicted. Therefore, if one is addicted to much wine, then they are an alcoholic. And as Jeff May brilliantly stated, "it doesn't take much to be addicted". There are many preachers who have said this same thing, but let's examine some statistics. According to a 2015 study conducted by the National Institute on Alcohol Abuse and Alcoholism (NIAAA), 29.1 percent of American adults misuse alcohol. The NIAAA also noted that 13.9 percent of American adults suffer from Alcohol Use Disorder (AUD). If you were told that you had even a 10% chance that your plane would crash after takeoff, would you risk taking the flight? Likewise, if you were told that you had a 14% chance of suffering from AUD and possibly falling into alcoholism, would you risk it?

In regards to the second claim, it should also be noted that just because the excess of one thing is forbidden, that doesn't necessarily mean that it is okay in smaller quantities. Take for example Ecclesiastes 7:17. In this passage, we have a warning by Solomon to avoid being "excessively wicked". What we need to understand is just because the excess of wickedness is condemned, that doesn't mean a little wickedness does no harm. Likewise, although one is not to be given to 'much wine', that doesn't mean a little wine is right.

The third claim that will be refuted is the one that puts Timothy as an example. "Timothy was told he could have a little wine, so that means it is okay for me too." There are some instances in which consuming wine is helpful and useful. The one and only instance in which alcohol is okay to use is if it is used to treat an ailment. In 1 Timothy 5:23, Paul instructs Timothy to use alcohol, but let us examine the entire passage.

> 1 Timothy 5:23
>
> *"Don't continue drinking only water, but use a little wine **because of your stomach and your frequent illnesses.**"* (CSB)

In scripture, there is only one reason given as to why one should consume wine. The only reason one should drink is if the alcoholic beverage is a treatment or cure to an illness. Oftentimes, this is used as an excuse by many to legitimize social drinking. If this was the case, then why did Timothy try so hard to avoid the consumption of alcohol in the first place? It is of personal opinion that Timothy and Paul understood the dangers of consuming wine, and they desired for it to only be consumed in certain cases and in small quantities.

Many try using the Greek and Hebrew languages to also try and legitimize the use of alcohol. I may not know enough about the Greek or Hebrew languages to contribute anything to that argument, but one thing I do know is that Christ would never be a stumbling block to others, and neither should we. If we are going to be living for Christ, we need to remove anything from our lives that would be a hindrance to serving Him.

DISCUSSION QUESTIONS

1. The Christian has been called to what kind of mind?

2. The scriptures tell of the dangers of alcohol and how it could be a hindrance to our salvation, but what other things could we be addicted to that would interfere with our salvation?

3. Would you be willing to risk your entire salvation on a drink that could possibly lead to an addiction and interfere with your walk with God?

4. If there is any hindrance in our walk with God, what should we do with it?

5
Little Calves

There are some things in our lives that just seem to get in the way of living for God. My youth minister when I was growing up would call these things "little idols". Some examples of these little idols are video games, sports, Netflix, etc. Sometimes we do not intend for things to get in the way of our walk with Him, but they do. However, other times, we intentionally give God the lesser place in our lives. I will refer to the things which we intentionally put in God's place as 'little calves'. Perhaps the best example of people intentionally putting away God in favor of something else can be found in Exodus 32.

In Exodus 32, the Hebrew people fell into the trap of intentionally putting things before God. In the 31st chapter, Moses ascended Mount Sinai to receive the commandments from the Lord. Moses was on the mountain for 40 days, but the people grew impatient with him and came to the false conclusion that he and God had abandoned them. Now in chapter 32, they sought to make other gods for themselves to lead them out of the wilderness. They convinced Aaron, the High Priest, to make a golden calf out of their golden jewelry. Not only did the people of Israel sin intentionally against God, but so did Aaron. Aaron could have ordered the conspirators to be put to death, but he let his position as High Priest get to his head and he intentionally put the people's interests before God's.

If we are to live for Christ, then we need to do so intentionally. Not only that, but we need to put Christ before other things, not the other way around. Look at Hebrews 2 has to say on intentionally keeping Christ first in our lives:

> Hebrews 2:1-4
>
> "Therefore **we must pay much closer attention to what we have heard**, lest we drift away from it. For since the message declared by angels proved to be reliable, and every transgression or disobedience received a just retribution, how shall we escape if we **neglect** such a great salvation? It was declared at first by the Lord, and it was attested to us by those who heard, while God also bore witness by signs and wonders and various miracles and by gifts of the Holy Spirit distributed according to his will." (CSB)

In this passage, there is one word that sticks out to me more than any other word, and that is 'neglect'. I believe and am convinced that there are two kinds of neglect one can have in regards to the Word revealed through Jesus Christ. The first kind of neglect is **unintentional neglect**. As was mentioned previously, this is putting things before God out of misplaced priorities. This kind of neglect is dangerous but can be fixed by reorganizing your schedule or by being more careful how you use your time. The other kind of neglect is **intentional neglect**. The Hebrew people in Exodus 32 intentionally neglected the will of God and there are many throughout scripture who do the same.

So as Christians, how can we avoid unintentionally neglecting our spirituality? Well, the author of Hebrews says that we have to 'pay much closer attention to what we have heard'. Now, I am not saying that just by listening we will automatically become more spiritual. However, if you are not intentionally listening and intentionally paying attention in Church, or if you are not intentionally reading your Bible and taking notes, it is going to be awfully hard to be intentional about your salvation and spirituality. I have seen all to often people leave the Church just because they just do not understand the Bible or why we do certain things as the Church; At the same time, I have seen many of these same people playing games on their electronic devices or sleeping as their questions and concerns are being addressed by teachers and preachers. I do not doubt their concerns, but I wonder how much better off they would be spiritually if they did not put other things before studying the Word of God. It is okay to have questions and concerns, but does one really care about their spirituality if they are not helping themselves by trying to find the answers to their concerns? This is a little calf that many need to overcome.

The next little calf I would like to address is sports and other extracurricular events. Think about it. How many children or teens in your congregation do not show up Sunday or Wednesday night because of sports' practices or other events? I know this was a big problem in my congregation growing up. And I have to admit, as an athlete in High School, I have been guilty of this myself. And I often wonder how much more I would know if I did not miss some of the youth group devotionals or teens' classes. Luckily, I had parents who really tried to ensure that I went to Church services and functions as often as possible, but it does not seem to be the same way in other families. I know of families who seem to use athletics and other extracurricular activities as excuses for why they should not show up Sunday or Wednesday night. This neglect, though it may be unintentional to begin with, could lead to one questioning if the Church is even really necessary, thus leading to future intentional neglect.

Christians have been called to worship God in Spirit and in Truth (John 4:23-24). In order to do this, we must intentionally strive to better ourselves by listening and personal study. We should not neglect Him by focusing on little calves, rather we should give Him first place in everything (Col. 1:18).

DISCUSSION QUESTIONS

1. What are some little calves (idols) that exist in your life?

2. How can you destroy some of these calves?

3. How can you personally better yourself by being intentional about your salvation?

4. Write John 4:23-24 below or write it on a separate sheet of paper:

5. What does it mean to worship God in Spirit and in Truth?

6
Lingering in Our Comfort Zones

Imagine what it would be like being scared of everything that came in front of you. Just picture in your head what life would be like if it was lived in constant fear. Fear of loneliness. Fear of pain. Fear of sickness. Fear of abandonment. Fear of physical death. What would the quality of your life be if you constantly thought about and dwelled on these things? I'd argue that the quality of your life would not be all that great. The fear of all of these things would result in anxiety and depression. I can tell you, as one who has experienced both of these things, life is too short to be lived in either one of these things.

Oftentimes we try to escape our fears by placing ourselves in a bubble. This bubble is often referred to as our comfort zone. All of us have one, though they differ in size. Some people are more afraid to come out of the comfort zones than others. In chapter 12, we will address the need to jump out of our comfort zones. However, in this chapter, we need to discuss why so many let irrational fears keep them inside their comfort zones, though some of these fears may be legitimate. Then, we need to discuss why staying in our comfort zones can keep us from living for Christ.

Before we can dive into our comfort zones, I want us to first look at the comfort zone of Jonah. Many of us, even those of us who have not been to a church, have heard of or read the story of Jonah. But if you have not, let me give you a brief summary of what went down in the short four chapter book. God appeared to Jonah and He commanded Jonah to IMMEDIATELY go to Nineveh (the wicked capital of Assyria) and proclaim a message of repentance. Jonah decided that he was not going to obey the commands of God; instead, he decided to flee from God by catching a ship that was sailing to Tarshish.

As you probably are already know, it is impossible to flee from God. He will catch you. God sent a storm that violently shook the ship Jonah was on. The sailors were afraid and cast lots to figure out who was the reason for the winds and waves. The lots fell on Jonah and he was eventually cast into the sea. The Lord then sent a large fish to swallow Jonah. God mercifully spared Jonah's life by releasing him from the belly of the fish and Jonah went on to proclaim God's message of repentance.

There is much more that happened after this story, but there are some things we need to examine about this portion. Here are three things to consider:

1. Jonah had a comfort zone.

2. Jonah chose to linger in his comfort zone.

3. Jonah let his comfort zone get in the way of him obeying the commands of God.

As was stated earlier, we all have a comfort zone. Where there is fear, there is a comfort zone. However, we can choose to linger (as Jonah did) or we can choose to come out of the comfort zone. When God called Jonah to come out of the comfort zone and obey the commands of God, Jonah did not.

Now, what does lingering inside our comfort zone look like for the modern Christian? Well, that could be very subjective. Since comfort zones differ in size from person to person, it is difficult to say what constitutes as lingering inside. For example, what I am comfortable doing, other people might not be as comfortable or completely uncomfortable doing. I am comfortable with speaking in a pulpit or teaching a Bible class. However, I understand that public speaking is not for everyone and most people would probably be pretty uncomfortable with being asked to deliver a thirty minute message. God has blessed each and every one of us with talents. I have been blessed with enough conversational skills (though I am introverted) that I consider it a God-given talent. Each and every individual reading this book needs to understand that he/she has a talent.

Let us consider for a second a parable of three individuals who were given coins[2]. This parable can be found in Matthew 25:14ff. Each of the servants was entrusted with coins. They each had different amounts of coins, but one of them refused to invest what had been given to him. This individual did not seek to come out of his comfort zone and instead decided he was going to sit around and do nothing. When the master returned, the other two servants received a prize for their willingness to work and invest the coins that were given to

---

[2] Talents

them. However, the servant who did not invest his coin had his reward taken from him. Let us not be like this servant.

If you fear the Lord more than you fear anything else, then coming out of your comfort zone to satisfy the will of God should be no problem to you (see Chapter 12!). There is no such thing as a "side-line Christian." Every single Christian has been given a coin to do something. Your coin may be art, writing, public speaking, or even fixing cars. If you don't use your talent for the glory of God, well, you might want to start.

It takes a little effort and maybe even coming out of your comfort zone to live for Christ, but it is well worth it. As Christians, we cannot stay lingering in our comfort zones.

DISCUSSION QUESTIONS

1. What are some fears that keep you inside your comfort zone?

2. Do these fears keep you from using your talents for the glory of God? If so, why?

3. What are some talents that you possess? How can you use them to further God's Kingdom?

4. What do you think it means to be a "side-line Christian"?

7
Focusing on Self

I am going to be honest with you… I love myself. I really do. Sometimes I love myself too much and other times I don't love myself enough. Generally speaking, though, I do love myself. I hope each one of you who reads this book loves yourself. So when you read the following pages, I do not want you to think I am telling you to hate yourself, because I am not.

How should the Christian view themselves? By contrast, how should Christians not view themselves? In this chapter, I hope to answer both of these questions.

As already mentioned, I desire everyone to practice self-love. This is not a desire I alone possess, but also the Lord. Consider Mark 12:31 where Jesus defines the second greatest commandment.

> Mark 12:31
>
> *"The second [greatest command] is, Love your neighbor as yourself. There is no command greater than these."* (CSB)

Jesus commands His disciples (followers) to love others as much as they love themselves. We will discuss more about how we love others in a later chapter, but I want to discuss briefly the "as yourself" portion of this verse. The fact that Jesus commands us (his followers) to love others as we love ourselves implies a command of self-love. One thing that love does not do is neglect. If we neglect to take care of ourselves or our bodies, then we are not giving ourselves enough love. If we are going to be 'living for Christ,' then we need to make an effort to keep on living while we can. So it is important that we do maintain love for ourselves.

But how much is too much? **Our love for self MUST not exceed or love for God or our love for others**. Today's society does not teach this. Therefore we need to discuss **denying self**.

Probably the best example within scripture of someone who denied self to further God's will as well as to save us was Jesus Christ. Since Jesus was a perfect human, being both divine and man, no better example can ever be put forth. Jesus not only taught denying self, he lived it out. Consider what Paul has to say in Philippians 2:5-8.

> Philippians 2:5-8
>
> *"Adopt the same attitude as that of Christ Jesus, who existing in the form of God, did not consider equality with God as something to be exploited. Instead he emptied himself by assuming the form of a servant, taking on the likeness of humanity. And when he had come as a man, he humbled himself by becoming obedient to the point of death - even to death on a cross."* (CSB)

Paul (through the Holy Spirit) commands the church in Philippi to "adopt the same attitude as that of Christ Jesus." One of the things that Christ had to do in order to assume the role of a servant was empty Himself - in other words, deny Himself. Christ even states in Matthew 20:28 that He did not come to be served, but to serve. Such humility and servitude can be seen in the life of Christ - just one more reason why we should live for Him. Through Christ's humility and servitude, we see a clear picture of God's love for humanity. As will be discussed later, denying oneself is the first step to loving others more.

Another great example within scripture of an individual who denied himself is Paul. As a matter of fact, we can attribute Paul's radical transformation in part to his decision to deny himself. This, again, can be seen in his epistle to the Philippians.

> Philippians 3:7
>
> *"But everything that was a gain to me, I have considered to be a loss because of Christ."* (CSB)

As was mentioned in the first chapter, Paul's life previous to his conversion would have made many of his Jewish counterparts envious - he was a Hebrew of Hebrews. However, Paul had to reject Saul. Paul had to reject, in a literal sense, who he was so that the gospel could shine through him. Paul understood that in order to live for Christ, he had to stop living for self. Did Paul hate himself? Absolutely not. He kept a physician with him (Luke) to make sure his body was in good shape, and he almost always had close friends and companions with him to ensure that his mental and spiritual health was in good shape.

If we are going to be people who are living for Christ, we should focus less on ourselves. Great alternatives are given in Chapters 9 and 11!

DISCUSSION QUESTIONS

1. Is it important to love yourself?

2. Go to Mark 12 and read vv. 30-31. What are the first and second greatest commands?

3. What are the two things our love for self must not exceed?

4. Aside from Paul and Jesus, what is another example (biblical or current) of someone who denied his/her self?

5. In the space below or on another sheet of paper, write Philippians 2:5-8 and describe how you can adopt the attitude of Christ.

8
Dying to Sin

People sin. Everybody does eventually. The Bible makes this very clear, particularly in Romans 3:23. In the second chapter of this book, the dangers of sin and its consequences were discussed. The biggest consequence of sin is eternal death. Because of sin entering this world, physical death is all but certain. But what about eternal death? If all sin, can one even escape eternal death if that is the consequence? One can avoid eternal death by accepting (via baptism) and obeying the Gospel. That is the one hope of salvation.

However, there is a statute within the Gospel that many often overlook. They like the part of the Bible that talks about God's love, the sacrifice of Jesus on a cross, and what it means to love one another; but they often overlook the part where we are told to die to our sins. Dying to our sins literally means to stop the wrong lifestyle and deeds we originally did, and to turn to Christ.

What all does dying to sin entail? Hopefully by the end of this chapter, I can effectively explain why we need to die to sin and maybe even discuss some practical ways we can do this.

We first need to discuss what dying to sin entails. Let us consider the state of Christians previous to their salvation, which can be found in Ephesians 2:1-2. This passage not only applies to the Christians who were in Ephesus, but to everyone as a whole. Since we have all sinned and fallen short of the glory of God, we were all dead (spiritually speaking) in our trespasses and sins.

There is a big difference between dying in sin and dying to sin. If one is dead **IN** sin, then spiritual death is the current state of the one living in a sinful lifestyle. Someone who is dead in sin has either not received the Gospel or not repented (turned away) from their sins. The covering of the sinner is sin, not the life-giving blood of Jesus Christ. If someone is dead **TO** sin, then death is the current state of the sinful lifestyle - not the sinner. Someone who is dead to sin has been covered with the blood of Christ and has made the decision to live a radically different life. Someone who is dead to sin has turned away from evil and is making a conscious effort to do right. There is a big difference. Let's consider what Paul has to say in Romans 6:1-4.

> Romans 6:1-4
>
> *"What should we say then? Should we continue in sin so that grace may multiply? Absolutely not! How can we who died to sin still live in it? Or are you unaware that all of us who were baptized into Christ Jesus were baptized into his death? Therefore we were buried with him by baptism into death, in order that, just as Christ was raised from the dead by the glory of the Father, so we too may walk in newness of life."* (CSB)

As can be seen by this epistle, someone who has died to sin is striving not to continue in their sinful ways. Will there be slip-ups? For sure. However, with the Gospel we have grace. This grace must not be abused, but it is there in case we slip up. Someone who is dead to sin was baptized into the death of Christ, and has been raised to walk in **newness** of life. Dying to sin implies a new life.

So why do we need to die to sin? If we are not saved by our works but by our faith, then why do we need to change? I firmly believe that the answer to both of these questions can again be found in Romans 6:1-4. If someone has received the gospel by faith, then he or she has accepted the grace of God as a gift. However, this gift was not free. As my High School economics teacher repeatedly said, "There ain't such thing as free sandwiches." The gift of grace had to be bought by someone, and God bought it with the blood of His own son - Jesus Christ. This gift was bought once and for all (Heb. 10:10) and to continue in sin is to neglect the gift given to us (Heb. 2:1-3). God is abundant in grace, but how much more should He have to give? God's grace cannot multiply more than it already has, because God already gave it all through His son. Now, in regards to being saved by our faith, we should realize that without **good works**, our faith becomes dead (James 2:17, 26). When we die to sin, good works should be what overtakes us. This is an outward sign of true repentance.

So how can we die to sin in a more practical manner? We of course begin the process by accepting the Gospel and by being physically baptized in water; but beyond that how do we go about living a repentant life? The best way for me to answer this is by saying this... it depends on the sin and the sinner. Everyone has their own struggles and everyone struggles differently. So I want to address a few sins in particular and how one can go about putting them away. These will not be covered completely in depth, but I hope some of my insights can help you to continue walking in newness of life.

Sin #1 - Sexual Immorality

This is one that most people probably struggle with. This is also probably one of the most difficult addictions anyone can overcome. Paul offers great practical advice in regards to overcoming sexual immorality and it can be found in 1 Corinthians 6:18. This advice - **Flee** sexual immorality. In a world and culture where sexual immorality seems to be shoved down our throats, avoiding sexual immorality may seem impossible. However, by avoiding certain settings in which sexual immorality is advertised or promoted, or keeping Christian friends close by in more open settings, we can hold ourselves more accountable.

Sin #2 - Anger

Even if I had twenty hands, I would not be able to count on all those fingers how many times I have had feelings of anger or hatred. This is one of my biggest struggles because I tend to internalize my own anger. If you are someone who struggles with this, I recommend either a destresser (such as a stress ball, or a healthy activity to clear your mind) or a therapist. It is okay have feelings of anger, but it is not okay to act in a sinful manner on your anger (Eph. 4:26) nor is it okay to fully vent your anger to someone else (Prov. 29:11). Instead, seek help and guidance before acting or reacting.

Sin #3 - Gluttony

Society has normalized the sin of gluttony. "If it feels good, do it." "If you want it, buy it." Having things is not a sin, but putting or cherishing things over God is gluttony and idolatry. Jesus gives some great practical advice to overcoming gluttony, but it is up to us to accept it. In Mark 10:17, a rich young ruler confronts Christ and he asks what he must do to inherit eternal life. He has already kept the law from his youth, but Christ states that the rich young ruler still lacks one thing: he needs to sell all that he has and give to the poor. The rich young ruler was given a choice: follow God or remain in his gluttonous life-style. He chose the latter. We can avoid the sin of gluttony by giving more and keeping less. There is so much more to life than collecting things. I recommend striving towards a minimalistic lifestyle.

Sin #4 - Harsh Words

There are so many different sins that could fall into this category. I would argue that most people (if not all) have cussed, cursed, or gossiped at some point in our lives. Some of us might be more used to doing it or hearing it than others. The sins of cursing and cussing especially has been normalized by today's world. I would argue that this normalization has helped encourage individuals who struggle with it to keep it as a habit. As with any bad habits or addictions, these can be difficult to break. One book I highly recommend is *The Power of Habit* by Charles Duhigg. Christians should be mindful of the words that they speak and how they can affect others (see James 3 and Colossians 4:6).

DISCUSSION QUESTIONS

1. What is the difference between being 'dead in sin' versus 'dead to sin'?

2. What does it mean to 'walk in newness of life'?

3. Why do we need to die to sin?

4. In this chapter, there are four sins that are covered that we need to die to. There are practical ways given to overcoming these sins. What are **other sins** that you may struggle with that you need to die to? What are some practical ways you can overcome them?

9

Chasing Christ

In the third chapter of this book, we discussed the dangers of chasing riches. However, I would like to discuss a better alternative - *chasing Christ*! The title of this chapter might seem kind of cliche, and it is definitely something that you might see in more modern Christian books. Nonetheless, we can not say we live for Christ if we do not chase after Him. But wait a second... Christ is not here on this earth anymore. How on earth are we supposed to chase Christ if He no longer dwells here? In this chapter, I want to answer both the why and the how.

Why should we want to chase Christ as opposed to the material things of this world? If we read Paul's letter to the Colossians, we can certainly find the answer to this question. Paul gives a quite lengthy (and poetic) description of why Christ is worthy of all of our focus and all of our attention in the first chapter. Let's focus our attention, however, on the 18th verse.

> Colossians 1:18
>
> *"He is also the head of the body, the Church; he is the beginning, the firstborn of the dead, so that he might come to have first place in everything."* (CSB)

In this passage, we read that Christ is head of the Church - the body of Christ. After His role as "the head" is mentioned, two additional qualifiers are given as to why He is the central figure of Christian worship.

The first qualifier given is that Christ is "the beginning". In other words, Christ existed before and during creation (see also Jn. 1:2 and Rev. 22:1). The second qualifier is that Jesus was "the firstborn of the dead." Jesus Christ, by his own divine power, raised himself from the dead. No one else in history has ever raised himself from the dead, but Christ did. And He did so three days after his death, proving the validity of the miracle. By being the firstborn of the dead, Jesus defeated death, which is the primary enemy of mankind (1 Cor. 15:26).

Special attention should be given, however, to the last part of this verse: "*... so that he might come to have first place in everything.*" Because Christ is the beginning and because He was raised from the dead after being crucified for our sins, He is worthy of worship. Not only that, but Christ deserves to have first place in EVERYTHING. The value of material items and riches should pale in comparison to what can be found in Christ Jesus.

So Christ is worthy of having first place, but what does it mean to 'chase Christ'? I would argue that there are three main ways we can pursue Christ outside of a worship context:
- Practicing spiritual disciplines
- Thinking Christ-like
- Being Christ-like

These will all be described in further detail. I can guarantee that if you follow all three of these, you will be Chasing Christ and that He will be chasing you! Are you willing?

Practicing Spiritual Disciplines:

If one does not practice spiritual disciplines, then discipleship becomes increasingly difficult. What are spiritual disciplines? **Spiritual disciplines** are behaviors or practices that help us grow spiritually and enable us to strive closer to spiritual maturity. Spiritual disciplines can be things as simple as prayer or Bible study. On the other hand, they can be difficult practices such as journaling, fasting, or meditation. Disciplines are not just experiences or emotions you feel; rather, they are practices that help you to be a better Christian - a Christ chaser. Some of these disciplines are essential to the faith and for salvation (i.e. praying), others are just good practices that can help one grow spiritually (i.e. journaling).

See also: 1 Thess. 1:2; 5:17; Acts 17:11; 2 Cor. 9:6; Matt. 6:16-18.

Thinking Christ-like:

"Cogito, ergo sum." In English, this is translated as *"I think, therefore I am."* This was a statement made by Rene Descartes in the midst of his own internal personal conflict. He doubted his very existence in the universe. However, he eventually came to the conclusion that because he has rational thoughts then he must exist. Can this somewhat apply to the Christian? I think so.

If we (Christians) think Christ-like thoughts, then we more closely identify with Christ. Since Christ is the author of our salvation (Hebrews 1:1-2), and He authored it by living a sinless life and by dying a sacrificial death, wouldn't it make sense then to model our thoughts and our attitudes after His? Disciples of Jesus Christ, therefore, need to model their thoughts after the thoughts of Christ. Otherwise, we lose our identity.

See also: Phil. 2:4ff; 2 Cor. 1:4-5; 1 John 1:5.

Being Christ-like:
In order to be Christ-like, we must not only think, we must do. However, we need to understand that no matter how hard we try, we will NEVER reach absolute perfection through our own works. After all, it is the blood of Christ that had to cover our sins and errors.

If a Christian is someone who belongs to Christ, then our actions should model His. I am not talking about actions such as performing miracles, but rather walking His walk and talking His talk. It is putting Christ's thoughts into action. *Cogito, ergo sum.* Jesus did good works to others by giving to the poor. He also did good works towards God by dedicating His whole life in service and devotion to Him. Jesus Christ practiced and taught spiritual disciplines because He also had to set an example for how we are to grow spiritually.

Being like Christ is the most important thing a disciple can do. This is how we keep our identity and how we truly chase Christ.

See also: 1 John 1:6-10; Heb. 12:1-2; Gal. 5:22ff; Matt. 28:20.

DISCUSSION QUESTIONS

1. What can you do differently in your life that will make you more of a Christ-chaser?

2. In order to chase Christ, what kind of things must we first put away?

3. What is a spiritual discipline that you could improve upon or add to your daily routine?

4. *Cogito, ergo sum.* Discuss.

5. Why would chasing Christ be a better alternative to chasing riches or other worldly things?

10
Consuming God's Word

Earlier on in the book, the dangers of consuming alcoholic beverages were discussed. In this chapter, I would like to discuss a better alternative - consuming God's Word! Just like Chapter 4, I would like for us to start in Hebrews 5:13-14.

> Hebrews 5:13-14
>
> *"Now everyone who lives on milk is inexperienced with the message about righteousness, because he is an infant. But solid food is for the mature - for those whose senses have been trained to distinguish between good and evil."* (CSB)

A Christian should desire to know the difference between good and evil. One of the dangers of alcoholic beverages that was discussed was the fact that it interferes with the training of our senses to distinguish between good and evil. However, if we strive to study God's Word more, then our senses have an opportunity to be trained and our minds have an opportunity to become more knowledgable.

Consuming God's Word has many more benefits than just adding to our knowledge, and as we move through this chapter, we will examine many of these benefits. Bible study is indeed one of the most important spiritual disciplines a Christian can and must practice!

Back when Paul wasn't a Christian and when he went by the name Saul, even then he understood the importance of studying the Scriptures. After all, he was educated by one of the greatest Jewish teachers at the time - Gamaliel. Even after his conversion from Judaism to Christianity, he knew that knowledge of the Scriptures was important. In Paul's last extant letter to Timothy, this is made even more evident.

> 2 Timothy 3:16-17
>
> *"All Scripture is inspired by God and is profitable for teaching, for rebuking, for correcting, for training in righteousness, so that the man of God may be complete, equipped for every good work."* (CSB)

Not only is God's Word inspired (or breathed out) by God, but it is profitable for many things such as the work of ministry and equipping the saints. As Christians, we should eat this stuff up. **Studying the Word of God should not have to be a chore, it should be a privilege.** Consider what Peter writes in 1 Peter 2.

> 1 Peter 2:2-3
>
> *"Like newborn infants, desire the pure milk of the word, so that you may grow up into your salvation, if you have tasted that the Lord is good."* (CSB)

It might seem a bit ironic that the author of Hebrews wants Christians to move from milk to solid food, but Peter wants Christians to desire the milk. The analogy isn't what Christians should be focused on, but rather the idea of growth. We need to move on from infancy and into maturity, and we do so by studying God's Word.

Not only are there commands in scripture concerning Bible study, there are also examples of adequate Bible study. Consider the Bereans in Acts 17:11 who "received the word with eagerness and examined the scriptures daily to see if [things being taught] were so." Often times, we are used to just hearing what the preachers have to say during worship or devotionals. And although we do want to receive the Word of God with eagerness, it is imperative that we are being taught honestly. **We have to ensure that what others teach us matches the scriptures.**

Another great example of adequate Bible study can be found in Acts 2:42. The first Christian converts are described as "devoting themselves to the apostles' teaching." The apostles taught exactly what Jesus Christ had taught (Matt. 28:20). Therefore, like the first-century Church, we should strive to follow the commands of Jesus Christ and His apostles.

[There are many books that exist on how the Bible came to be and how Christians are to rightly divide the Word of Truth (see 2 Tim. 2:15). Two books I highly recommend are *How We Got the Bible* by Neil R. Lightfoot and *Bible Bytes 1.0* by Daren Schroeder.]

DISCUSSION QUESTIONS

1. Do you think you study the Scriptures as much as you should? Why or why not?

2. What can you do to better improve your Bible study?

3. Read 1 Peter 3:15. Please explain why Bible study is important if we want to be able to give a defense.

4. Besides adding to our knowledge, what are some other benefits of Bible study?

11

Focusing on Others

In contrast to what was discussed in Chapter 7 (focusing on ourselves), I would like for us to now cover the better option - focusing on others. This might seem like an easy task, but if we have the wrong attitude in life, then it isn't. Focusing on others was something that Jesus Christ did and it is something that we must also do (see p. 37). As a matter of fact, Jesus Christ is the prime example we will be looking at in this chapter in regards to why and how we should focus on others.

Consider John 3:16.

> John 3:16
>
> *"For God loved the world in this way: He gave his one and only Son, so that everyone who believes in him will not perish but have eternal life."* (CSB)

This passage has been widely regarded as "The Gospel in a Nutshell." God had so much love for this world that He sent Jesus Christ so that we can have hope. God did not have to show mercy or grace, but He did it out of love. Likewise, when we talk about focusing on others, we need to understand that we do so because God first loved us (1 John 3-4). We need not only focus on others in delivering the Gospel to them, we need to show them love and compassion through good works. We need to be holistic Christians. Jesus was the model of a holistic servant who focused on others' needs rather than his own.

In Mark 6:30, we read of five thousand people who had followed Jesus. These people all ran on foot to hear and meet the Messiah, but they did not have time to eat. They were not only hungry for the Word, they were also hungry for food. Jesus Christ understood this. Read what v. 34 has to say.

> Mark 6:34
>
> *"When he went ashore, he saw a large number and had compassion on them, because they were like sheep without a shepherd. Then he began to teach them many things."* (CSB)

Jesus didn't end with just teaching and preaching to the people. Beginning in v. 37, we read the miracle of Jesus feeding five thousand people with five loaves and two fish! We could just say that the role of the Church is to spread the gospel to other people. However, Jesus understood the importance of focusing on both the spiritual and physical needs of everyone. Compassion and love defined the ministry of Jesus and it needs to define our dealings with others.

In Philippians 2, Paul talks about another attitude Christ possessed when dealing with others. In v. 4, Paul charges everyone to not look out only for their own interests, but for the interests of others. This is called humility (see v. 3). This has already been covered in Chapter 7, but this must not be forgotten. We need to remember that in caring for others, we are not shining, but God is. We are just servants of God hoping to make more servants.

Throughout the New Testament, we see several passages about giving to the poor, helping the physically impaired, caring for widows and orphans, etc. All of these actions are focused on other individuals, not ourselves. In James 1:27, we see a great passage on what it means to practice "true religion." The definition of **true religion**, according to James, is to look after orphans and widows in their distress and to keep oneself unstained from the world. If we do not care for others, how can we call ourselves Christians? Christ cared for others, therefore we should too. Therefore we should do what the Word of God says and not only look after our own spiritual well-being, but the well-being of others.

God didn't just begin requiring caring for others in the New Testament era. Even the Jews under the Old Law were instructed to give to the poor and care for others in need. The Old Law has often been labeled as a collection of books that describe God's hatred and wrath. However, this is not the case. There are many passages within the Old Testament that describe not only God's love for his people, but also instructions in regards to dealing with others. Some passages that talk about how to treat others include: Proverbs 3:27; 11:17, 25; 12:26; 15:1; 28:27; Deut. 15:10-11; Ex. 17:12; Is. 53:4-5.

We need to put on love and humility in order to be wholesome individuals. When I was in High School, I oftentimes wondered why no one talked to me. Then I came to understand that the only way to attract people to myself was to try to show them the same love and humility I have been shown by God. Likewise, if we want to be a holistic Church, we need to put on love and humility for the people in the world outside of it.

DISCUSSION QUESTIONS

1. Do you feel as if you care for the needs of others?

2. What is another example of Christ that you can think of in regards to how he dealt with others? It can be a miracle of some sort or a teaching.

3. What is true (pure) religion?

4. Love and humility are two attitudes needed for holistic work in the church. Can you think of any other attitudes Christians should have in dealing with others?

12

Jumping Out of Our Comfort Zones

Jonah lived in his comfort zone, but we should do the opposite. We must be willing to live outside of our comfort zones. The life of the Christian must not be lived in fear, but in courage and full dedication. The life and ministry of Paul was one lived outside of the comfort zone. He strived to model Christ in his living, therefore we can also say that Christ lived His life outside of the comfort zone. If we are to imitate Paul as he imitated Christ (1 Cor. 11:1), then we need to be willing (and have the faith) to go above and beyond. There are many areas of life and ministry in which the members of the Church can get out of their comfort zones. Most of these will be discussed further.

The first area I would like to discuss is missions. Being a Bible Missions major at Freed-Hardeman University, and being someone who has the desire to take the gospel to Europe, I would say that this is an area that I am pretty passionate about. However, it seems that this area is one that most people are afraid of. As was mentioned in Chapter 6, each and every Christian has been given particular talents. I understand (and so does God) that not everyone has the talent of conversational evangelism. In addition, not everyone desires to move to a place for an extended period of time. But let us consider what Paul has to say in Romans 1:16.

> **Romans 1:16**
>
> *"For I am not ashamed of the gospel, because it is the power of God for salvation to everyone who believes, first to the Jew, and also to the Greek."* (CSB)

For Paul, he was not ashamed of the gospel because he understood that it was the power behind salvation. Therefore when Paul is taking the gospel to people all throughout the Roman Empire, he does not fear man because what can they do to him (see Psalm 118:6)? Kill him? Paul did not fear death because heaven would have been his reward (2 Cor. 5). Torture him? The Jewish and Roman authorities tried that - didn't faze him. Judge him? They did. He was not a great speaker nor a man of fine appearance. Nonetheless, he preached the gospel (2 Cor. 10-11). We must be willing to do the same, regardless if we are located (permanent) missionaries abroad, or sharing the message with others around us in our own native environment. We must be willing to give other people the gospel, because it is the power for their salvation. Regardless of how awkward or dangerous it may be.

The second area of coming out of our comfort zones I would like to discuss is doing good works. This is something that we talked a little bit about in the eleventh chapter, but it is always good to have another reminder! Especially in an era where all people want to do is be "entertained" in a worship service, the idea of doing good to and for others has become foreign. This is because people have forgotten to apply scriptures and teachings to their daily lives. In order to come out of our comfort zones, we need to be willing to apply the scriptures to ourselves. In Galatians, Paul was dealing with a church overcome with legalism and tradition. It becomes apparent in Paul's letter that the congregation had neglected to do good to others and wanted to remain in a comfort zone. However, Paul called them out of the comfort zone by saying, "let us work for the good of all, especially for those who belong to the household of faith."

The third area that will be discussed is the area of discipleship. Being a disciple of Christ means being a follower of Christ. However, how far are we willing to follow Christ? Are we willing to follow Christ to our graves? Consider what Jude writes in his epistle.

> Jude 20
>
> *"But you, dear friends, as you build yourselves up in your most holy faith, praying in the Holy Spirit, keep yourselves in the love of God, waiting expectantly for the mercy of our Lord Jesus Christ for eternal life."* (CSB)

Jude says that we are to keep ourselves in the love of God. If we depart from the faith, how are we to remain in the love of God? God requires faith, and remaining in His love is the result. In Revelation, Jesus states that Christians are to "be faithful to the point of death." It is possible to fall from God's grace if we are not faithful throughout the rest of our lives after conversion.

There are many other areas of the Christian faith that call for Christians to come out of their comfort zone. These three, though, were probably the ones that needed to be discussed the most. If we do not want to be a Jonah, then we need to jump out of our comfort zones. If we do not want to be a coward, then we need to jump out of our comfort zones. Doing this will make us stronger. No one has ever increased or built up their faith by being complacent in their comfort zone. It has only been accomplished by trials and the testing of our faith (James 1:2-4).

DISCUSSION QUESTIONS

1. What about this chapter was encouraging to you? Why?

2. Did any part of this chapter 'shock' you or make you uncomfortable? Why?

3. Why was Paul never ashamed of the gospel?

4. Which one of these three areas do you think affects you or speaks to you the most?

13

Your Radical Change

Hopefully, by now, you have seen a glimpse of what it means to live. For the Christian, the meaning of life should be Christ. Paul's love for Christ led to a radical change within himself. Paul no longer lived for himself, but he lived to please God and to bring others to Him. If you have your Bible open as you are going through this book, I ask that you please highlight this passage - Galatians 2:20.

> Galatians 2:20
>
> *"I have been crucified with Christ, and I no longer live, but Christ lives in me. The life I now live in the body, I live by faith in the Son of God, who loved me and gave himself for me."* (CSB)

When Paul became a Christian, the radical change was instantaneous. I wish I changed as radically as Paul did at his conversion (note the conversion in Acts 9, then him immediately proclaiming the gospel in v. 20). Paul crucified himself with Christ. He crucified everything about his past life - his sins, what he took pleasure in, and what he taught. Christ became the message in his body and in his words.

Does our radical change look anything like this? Can we say that after our conversion we tried to imitate, teach, or learn more about the gospel? Hopefully by accepting the gospel via baptism, you have decided that you will die to your sins rather than in your sins. Hopefully you have decided that you will chase Christ and not riches or physical pleasures. Hopefully you have decided that you will consume God's word and try to discern between good and evil, and not give into the temptation of a drink that can interfere with it. Do you want to linger in your comfort zone? It is my hope that you come out of your comfort zone. Do you want distractions? Hopefully you want to please God rather than men. Lastly, I hope you do good to others as God has done good unto you.

Paul taught and followed all of these principles, so that hopefully he could bring others to live for Christ. Do this as Paul did this. If you do this, I promise that your life will be more fulfilling and more purposeful.

NOTES

APPENDIX

Exegetical Approach to Philippians 1:20-30

** Taken from an essay I did at Freed-Hardeman University in fulfillment of my Biblical Exegesis class. I have included this article because it can help shed some light on Paul's bold statement in Philippians 1:21. **

Paul's epistle to the Philippians is often viewed as one of joy and thankfulness, the source of Paul's joy being Christ Jesus. This fulfillment and joy Paul finds in Christ is perhaps most evident within Philippians 1:20-30. In this pericope, Christians can find the meaning of life and can come to a deeper appreciation of the sacrifices made by Christ and his apostles. However, the text must be properly understood in order for it to be fully appreciated by and applied to the Christian in a modern setting. Before a proper examination of Philippians 1:20-30 can be made, it must first be quoted in its entirety, without pauses or interruptions. Philippians 1:20-30 reads as follows:

> [20]*My eager expectation and hope is that I will not be ashamed about anything, but that now as always, with all courage, Christ will be highly honored in my body, whether by life or by death.* [21]*For me, to live is Christ and to die is gain.* [22]*Now if I live on in the flesh, this means fruitful work for me; and I don't know which one I should choose.* [23]*I am torn between the two. I long to depart and be with Christ - which is far better -* [24]*but to remain in the flesh is more necessary for your sake.* [25]*Since I am persuaded of this, I know that I will*

remain and continue with all of you for your progress and joy in the faith, ²⁶so that, because of my coming to you again, your boasting in Christ Jesus may abound. ²⁷Just one thing: As citizens of heaven, live your life worthy of the gospel of Christ. Then, whether I come and see you or am absent, I will hear about you that you are standing firm in one spirit, in one accord, contending together for the faith of the gospel, ²⁸not being frightened in any way by your opponents. This is a sign of destruction for them, but of your salvation - and this is from God. ²⁹For it has been granted to you on Christ's behalf not only to believe in him, but also to suffer for him, ³⁰since you are engaged in the same struggle that you saw I had and now hear that I have. (CSB 2017)

This passage carries with it a very heavy meaning. This meaning can only have an impact on its readers if the context surrounding it is examined properly. Twenty-first century readers need to empty their minds of twenty-first century culture and reasoning(s), and step into the shoes of first-century Christians in the city of Philippi. Before this is done, an understanding of the author, culture of Philippi, and literary context must be developed.

Authorship and Critical Issues

The epistle to the Philippians was authored by Paul and coauthored by Timothy. This is evident in the salutation (1:1). There is not much debate on the authorship Philippians, but much more focus is usually placed on its date of composition and the unity of its contents.

There are two long-standing stances on the dating of Philippians. The first (and more traditional) stance is that the letter was written at Rome during Paul's imprisonment, shortly before his execution in AD 62 or 64. Byzantine and Syriac manuscripts have a *subscriptio* following the letter which mentions Epaphroditus as the possible amanuensis or messenger of the letter. The second stance is that the letter was written east of Rome during one of Paul's other imprisonments in Ephesus or Caesarea - prior to his imprisonment in Rome (Nelson 177-178). For the purpose of this study, the more traditional stance will be assumed.

Another critical issue concerning Philippians has been the unity of the epistle. There are some that hold that Philippians is a combination of two letters (Nelson 175). This belief has very little backing and is only based on the supposedly awkward placement of Paul's admonitions and appeals in Philippians 4:2-9. For the purpose of this study, the unity of this epistle will also be assumed.

Context

The city of Philippi was a Roman colony and a leading city of Macedonia (cf. Acts 16:12). The name of the city has its origins from Philip of Macedon - father of Alexander the Great. Philippi was largely a gentile city and there is no record of a Jewish synagogue within it. It is believed that Philippi was the location of the first planted church in Europe. The Church at Philippi was founded around AD 50-51 and a brief account of its founding is located within Acts 16 (People's NT 208). Paul and Silas were thrown into prison in Philippi after having been beaten; but thanks to their Roman citizenship, they were released and continued their missionary journeys. Following his imprisonment in Rome up to the time of this letter's composition, the Philippian Church continued to be very supportive of Paul and his work.

When examining the literary context, the geographical context (above) must be kept in mind. John Ramsey, in his book *Cover to Cover*, states the following:
> *From a prison cell in Rome the great apostle pens an epistle of encouragement to brethren who had helped him constantly in the spread of the gospel "from the first day even until now."*

When Paul is writing this pericope, it must be understood that he is doing so with an attitude of thanksgiving and eagerness to visit his fellow saints in Philippi.

In verses 3-11, Paul states his thankfulness for the Church in Philippi for being his "partners [with Paul] in grace, both in [his] **imprisonment** and in the defense and confirmation of the gospel" (CSB). Not only does he miss the Philippians, he "longs after them with the affection of Christ Jesus" (CSB). In other words, he longs for their presence (Peoples NT 211). In verses 9-11, Paul makes a brief prayer that the Philippians will grow in their love, knowledge, and discernment. The Christians in Philippi do not have it easy, but the difficult circumstances they are faced with do not give them an excuse to be complacent or stagnant.

In verses 12-19, Paul transitions into another matter in hopes that the Christians in Philippi will be encouraged by his words. He focuses on the reason for his imprisonment - "because I [Paul] am in Christ" (CSB). Many of Paul's fellow 'brothers' had gained confidence because of Paul's chains, and as a result are less fearful of spreading the gospel (v.14). However, there are some brethren that have wrong motivations for preaching Christ; but nonetheless, Paul is happy because Christ is still being proclaimed (v.15-19).

If these passages are kept in mind when examining the selected pericope, then this study becomes more simple and the passage more clear.

The Passage - Key Words

Within this passage, there are a few words that require further examination in order to better grasp the intended meaning of Paul's letter. These are the Greek words that will be discussed and studied further: ζωή, θάνατος, σαρκὶ, and ἀξίως.

The first word that warrants further examination and study is ζωή. This word appears five times in this pericope - twice in noun form and thrice in verbal form (ζάω). This word simply means 'life' or 'to live'. This word can be taken in both the literal sense and the figurative sense (Strong's Exhaustive Concordance). When Paul is using this word in this passage, it seems to be used in both senses. He not only wants his life to represent Christ, he wants it to be a sacrifice pleasing to Christ.

The next word is an antonym to ζωή. θάνατος (noun form) or ἀποθνήσκω (verb form) means 'death' or 'to die'. In the twentieth and twenty-first verses, these words are used in contrast to one another. 'Living' is equated with Christ, and 'dying' is equated with gain.

σάρξ or σαρκὶ is perhaps one of the more difficult words in this passage. This Greek word is used twice in this pericope - in the twenty-second and twenty-fourth verses. Most translations render 'flesh'. Within the context of this passage, however, it would be most appropriate to render 'body'. This Greek word is used on numerous occasions to refer to a 'lifestyle of sin' or 'carrying out fleshly desires' (see Romans 8:3-12). This is not what Paul is referring to here. Instead, he is referring to a physical fleshly body. In v. 24, Paul states that it is necessary to remain in the flesh for the sake of the Philippians. If living in the flesh is condemned in Romans 8, then why is Paul saying that he desires to continue to remain in the flesh for the sake of the Philippians? It is because Paul is only referring to living in a physical body.

Many might overlook the significance of this next word, ἀξίως, in v. 27. This adverb translates to 'worthy' or 'worthily'. This adverb is modifying the word πολιτεύεσθε, meaning 'conducting yourselves'. So Paul is instructing the saints (here described as 'citizens of heaven') to conduct themselves worthily of the gospel of Christ.

The Passage - Interpretive Issues

A few interpretive issues have been identified throughout this study. Some of these translational issues and variants will be discussed to more fully grasp and understand the true intended meaning of the message.

The first of these interpretive issues can be found in verse 20. The NIV (dynamic equivalence) renders "sufficient courage" whereas the ESV (formal equivalence) renders "full courage". The CSB ('optimal' equivalence) maintains a more literal rendering with "all courage". The Greek word πάσῃ literally translates to 'all'. It occurs forty-five times and refers to *a complete or perfect whole* (Englishman's Concordance).

Another issue in regards to a word's interpretation can be found in verse 21. This is probably the most well-known verse within the selected pericope, but it is also probably the most abused and mistranslated. The more literal translations correctly translate this passage, whereas the dynamic equivalence translations fail in attempt to explain Paul's intended meaning. As a result, meaning is lost. The NASB (formal equivalence) renders this: "For to me, to live is Christ and to die is gain." More liberal translations such as the GNT and the NLT try to elaborate upon the meaning of 'gain'. However, this is an intentional ambiguity and should not be further elaborated upon. The Greek word for 'gain' is κέρδος. It is used only three times in the New Testament, two of which are in Paul's letter to the Philippians. The only other time κέρδος is used in scripture is in Titus 1:11 in reference to a profit or financial gain. However, in the context of Philippians, this is a more ambiguous term that does not need help in translation.

Relation to Other Passages

This passage is unique in many ways in that it demonstrates Paul's willingness to sacrifice himself for the sake of Christ in bringing many with him to glory. In this passage, readers can clearly identify what the definition of life was for Paul. However, this passage bears resemblance to other passages within Acts and some other letters of Paul.

A passage that sheds much light on this pericope is Acts 16:16-40. Paul and Silas were imprisoned in Philippi after having been beaten. While they were in the prison, they began singing and praying to God and their fellow prisoners listened to them. Luke records that there was a sudden earthquake and the chains of the prisoners came loose and their doors were opened. Paul and the other prisoners, however, continued to remain in prison rather than escape. The jailer (who had thought of killing himself) was converted by Paul. The magistrates who had Paul thrown into prison issued an official apology to him after learning of his Roman citizenship, and Paul departed from Philippi. How does this passage shed light on Philippians 1:20-30? Well, the saints at Philippi would hopefully immediately recall the sacrificial ministry of Paul within the city of Philippi. In v. 30, Paul describes the struggle they once heard he had and now had. The Christians in Philippi are well acquainted with Paul's struggles and even face persecutions of their own.

A couple other passages that shed light on Philippians 1:20-30 are Colossians 2:4 and Colossians 3:1-4 (Pulpit Commentary). Although the meanings differ in that these passages in Colossians have more to do with spiritual living then physical living, it is imperative to understand that both should revolve around Christ. Paul wants to magnify Christ through his life of sacrificial ministry and spiritual dedication.

Perhaps the best passage that can be used with this pericope is Romans 8:18. In this passage, Paul explains why the present groanings and sufferings cannot be compared to the glory that will be revealed in Heaven. This is the very idea

Paul is describing in Philippians 1:21 and 1:28-30. Suffering for Christ presently will result in salvation after this life.

Practical Application

The Philippians were facing trials of their own (1:30). Paul, who was facing the same trials and struggles, empathizes with the Philippians and attempts to encourage them by explaining the reasons for his ministry to them - so their boasting in Christ Jesus may abound (1:26). Paul then encourages the Philippians to live their life worthy of the gospel calling and to stand firm together - not being fearful of their opponents, but instead ready for their salvation.

Christians today can be encouraged by these words written by Paul over two thousand years ago. There are many Christians in the world who are facing physical persecution and trials as a result of their faith. However, the reason for continuing in the struggle is so that Christ may continue to abound. More 'passive Christians' can gain a calling with this passage and hopefully come to understand that Christ is truly worth living for, and that heaven is worth dying to get to.

Works Cited

Farrar, Frederic William, et al. *The Pulpit Commentary*. Hendrickson Publishers, 2011.

Grant, Frederick C. *Nelson's Bible Commentary: Vol. 7, New Testament, Romans-Revelation*. Nelson & Sons, 1962.

Johnson, Barton Warren. *The People's New Testament, the Common and Revised Versions, with References and Colored Maps. With Explanatory Notes by B.W. Johnson*. Gospel Advocate Co., 1955.

Strong, James. *Strong's Exhaustive Concordance: with Greek and Hebrew Dictionary*. Manna Publishers.

Wigram, George V. *The New Englishman's Greek Concordance of the New Testament*. Associated Publishers & Authors, 1976.

NOTES

NOTES

About the Author

Joshua Dykes was born on July 11th, 1999 in Montgomery, Alabama. His parents (Michael and Heather) have been faithful Christians for many years and have raised both of their sons in the Church. He was raised in Trussville, Alabama where he attended Hewitt-Trussville High School, graduating in 2017. Much of his teenage years, he and his family attended Roebuck Parkway church of Christ (now Deerfoot coC). Entering into his senior year of High School, he made the life-changing decision to enter into the ministry.

He currently is a senior at Freed-Hardeman University in Henderson, Tennessee. While at school, he also serves as the Associate Minister at Central church of Christ in Decaturville, Tennessee. His future plans are to move to Romania (and eventually Iceland) to be a missionary.

Made in the USA
Monee, IL
04 September 2021